## Reading Success Mini-Books

# INITIAL CONSONANTS

## Twenty Interactive Mini-Books That Help Every Child Get a Great Start in Reading

### by Mary Beth Spann

SCHOLASTIC
PROFESSIONAL BOOKS

New York ● Toronto ● London ● Auckland ● Sydney ● Mexico City ● New Delhi ● Hong Kong

Cover design by Jaime Lucero and Norma Ortiz

Interior design by Ellen Matlach Hassell
for Boultinghouse & Boultinghouse, Inc.

Illustrations by Rusty Fletcher

ISBN: 0-439-08678-7

# Contents

# Introduction

Welcome to *Reading Success Mini-Books: Initial Consonants.* This book provides a fun and easy way for young children to experience beginning consonant letters and sounds. When used as a regular part of a balanced approach to literacy—one that includes reading, writing, speaking, and listening—these mini-books will provide children with an easy-to-understand, concrete foundation for single consonant sound/symbol mastery.

Research tells us that children learn letter sounds best when they're presented in a meaningful context. Each initial consonant mini-book introduces children to a group of simple, illustrated words that feature the same initial consonant letter and letter sound. Each mini-book offers children the chance to practice writing and reading these words, and provides a simple review activity so children can test themselves on what they've learned.

The books' small size means they are a breeze for young students to complete, store, collect, and keep. They help give children a sense of mastery and ownership over the letters they are learning. In a way, these mini-books serve as children's own print-awareness progress reports. As children successfully work through the books, it's easy for them to see how each one represents an important step on the road to reading.

## *Assembling the Mini-Books*

1. Make a double-sided copy of the mini-book pages.

2. Cut the page in half along the solid line.

3. Place pages 4/5 on top of page 2/7 as shown.

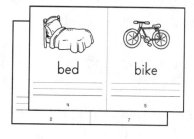

4. Fold the pages in half along the dotted line.

5. Check to be sure that the pages are in the proper order and then staple them together along the book's spine.

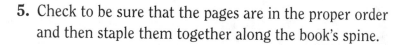

# How to Use This Book

This book contains 20 six-page mini-books—one book for each initial consonant letter sound in the English alphabet (with the exception of X). How you introduce and share these books with children will largely depend on how you introduce the beginning consonant sounds in general. But no matter how you choose to use them, you'll find these mini-books to be small, but powerful page-turners. Here are some ideas for putting them to work in your classroom:

## Pre-assemble Mini-Books as Needed

Instead of asking children to assemble these books in class, you may want to assemble a complete class set ahead of time. This prep-step allows students to focus their attention on the mini-books' content, rather than on construction. Remember: Parents who are unable to volunteer in the classroom may welcome this task as something they can work on at home.

## Let the Books Serve You

Here are some quick tips for making the mini-books as successful part of your reading routine:

- If you introduce alphabet letters in a particular sequence to the whole class, you might introduce the mini-books in that same sequence. Each student, or small groups of students, may then work on the same letter mini-book simultaneously.

- For an individualized approach, in which each child comes to know alphabet letters at his or her own rate, you may make the books available to children on an "as-needed" basis. Perhaps you can display an alphabet border at children's eye level, with a supply of mini-books stored in envelopes pinned beneath each consonant letter, or set up a consonant learning center, stocked with the mini-books. When individualizing, keep a mini-book checklist showing which ones each child has completed. Be certain to schedule student/teacher conferences so you can assess and celebrate children's progress.

- As children learn how to read and spell the words in the mini-books, consider transferring the words to word wall lists. Invite children to write and illustrate additional words for each list. Encourage children to refer to their mini-books and/or word walls when writing stories and books of their own.

## Recommended Read

In his comprehensive resource book, *Phonics From A to Z: A Practical Guide* (Scholastic Professional Books, 1998), reading expert Wiley Blevins recommends a phonics sequence for introducing letters and sounds. Because this must-have book offers explanations and rationales for all aspects of phonics instruction, it is very helpful in guiding the use of phonics mini-books.

# Introducing the Mini-Books in Class

1. Show children how a book is constructed and what they are expected to do on each page.

2. Work through one mini-book together.

   a. Read the cover together. Demonstrate how to use the "Name" line. Call attention to the configuration of the upper- and lower-case letters printed there.

   b. Call attention to the picture and word on each page. Focus children's attention on the print feature of each word by inviting them to share their decoding strategies.

   c. Demonstrate how to copy the word on the line provided. Suggest to children that if they think they already know how to spell the word, they can try and cover the word below the picture and write the word without peeking.

   d. Show how the back-cover activity serves as a self-checking review page. (Tip: The back cover can also serve as a screening page. If you suspect a child already knows how to read, spell, and write all the words in a mini-book, you can ask him or her to complete this page before completing the whole book. That way you'll know if the child needs to move on to a mini-book that is at a more appropriate instructional level.)

# Mini-Book Extensions

- Meet periodically with each student to review mini-books together. To organize their mini-book collections, give each child a large metal loose-leaf ring. Punch a hole in the upper left-hand corner of each completed mini-book and slip each one onto the ring. Store collections in a multi-pocketed shoe bag (hanging on a wall or from a doorknob), or hung on wall hooks.

- A tree trunk and branches decorated with a few paper leaves makes a nice bulletin-board backdrop for displaying new books (before adding them to the rings). Just tack individual books to the branches so they resemble leaves. Title your display "Leaf Through a Mini-Book!"

- Set aside class time for children to take turns sharing one book of their choice.

- Designate one day a week as "Mini-Book Take-Home Day" so children can share their growing library with family members.

- Provide blank mini-books so children can write and illustrate their own ideas. Children may want to compile initial-consonant mini-books with a theme (for example, *Foods Beginning with Letter G*). For inspiration, guide children to student dictionaries and nonfiction glossaries.

- Look for other opportunities to build awareness of initial consonants as they appear in literature and in the everyday world:
  - Go on letter walks, looking for signs featuring words beginning with a particular consonant.
  - Highlight initial consonants you find in newspaper and magazine ads, poetry, pocket chart selections, and stories.
  - Share books featuring titles and characters whose names begin with a particular target consonant.

## Generating Family Support

1. When familiarizing families with instructional materials and strategies you plan on using to teach reading and writing, introduce phonics mini-books as part of your overall approach.

2. Emphasize that a well-balanced program includes phonics plus many other strategies for reading, speaking, listening, and writing with children. Share specific examples of how you include these components in your program.

3. Invite families to extend learning at home by reading aloud together every day, by calling attention to the print that fills their days, and by reviewing school work—including mini-books—with their children.

## Match-up!

bike

ball

bed

bird

book

bag

8

# My Book of Words Beginning with Bb

Name _____

Reading Success Mini-Books: Initial Consonants    Scholastic Professional Books

I

# bird

6

# ball

3

# bag

2

# book

7

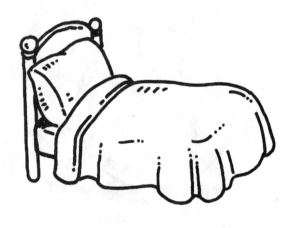

# bed

4

# bike

5

# Match-up!

can

cake

cow

cat

comb

car

# My Book of Words Begininng with Cc

Name _____

Reading Success Mini-Books: Initial Consonants    Scholastic Professional Books

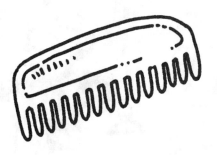

## comb

## can

# cake

_____
- - - - - - - - -
_____

2

# cow

_____
- - - - - - - - -
_____

7

# car

_____
_____
_____

4

# cat

_____
_____
_____

5

# Match-up!

dollar

desk

door

duck

dime

deer

8

# My Book of Words Beginning with Dd

*Reading Success Mini-Books: Initial Consonants*    Scholastic Professional Books

Name _____

1

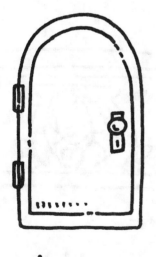

# door

6

# desk

3

# deer

_____

- - - - - - - - - - -

_____

2

# duck

_____

- - - - - - - - - - -

_____

7

# dime

_____

- - - - - - - - - - -

_____

4

# dollar

_____

- - - - - - - - - - -

_____

5

## Match-up!

fish

fan

feather

fence

fox

fork

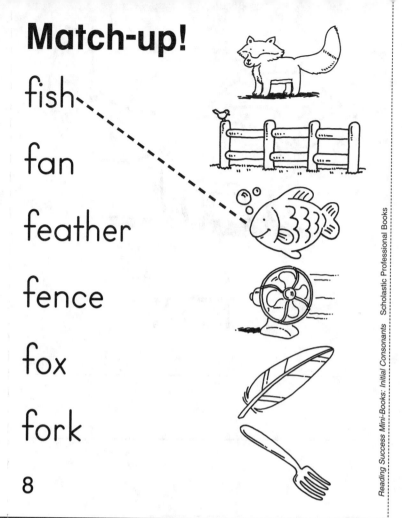

8

Reading Success Mini-Books: Initial Consonants    Scholastic Professional Books

# My Book of Words Beginning with Ff

Name _____

1

## fork

6

## feather

3

# fan

2

# fox

7

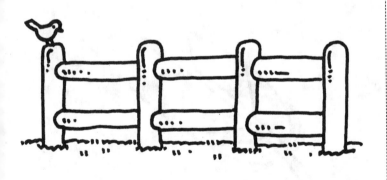

# fence

4

# fish

5

## Match-up!

gift

game

gate

guitar

goose

gum

8

Name _____

1

*Reading Success Mini-Books: Initial Consonants*   Scholastic Professional Books

## guitar

_____

_____

6

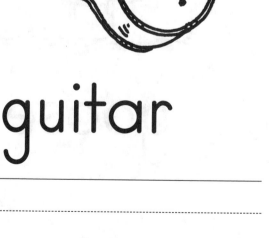

## gate

_____

_____

3

# game

---

2

# gum

---

7

# gift

---

4

# goose

---

5

# Match-up!

hippo

hat

hammer

hair

home

heart

8

# My Book of Words Beginning with **Hh**

Name _____

1

# home

6

# hat

3

# hammer

---

2

# hair

---

7

# heart

---

4

# hippo

---

5

## Match-up!

juice

jump

jacket

jar

jet

jeans

8

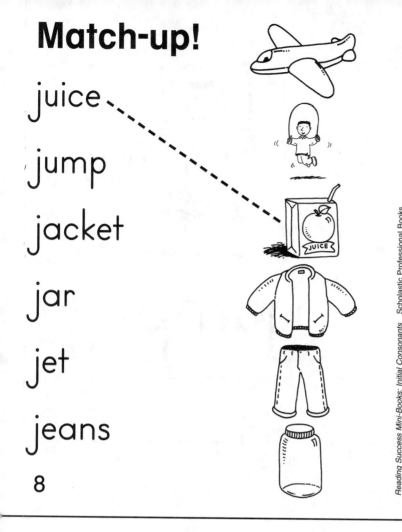

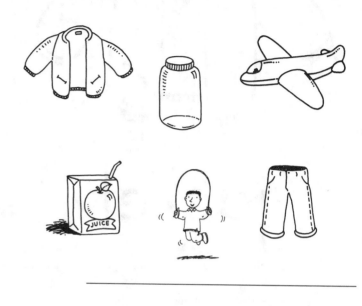

Name _____

1

*Reading Success Mini-Books: Initial Consonants*   Scholastic Professional Books

# juice

_____

6

# jar

_____

3

# jacket

2

# jump

7

# jeans

4

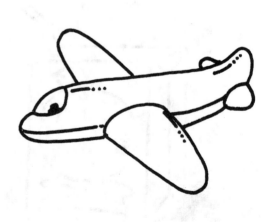

# jet

5

# Match-up!

kite

kettle

kitten

king

kiss

kangaroo

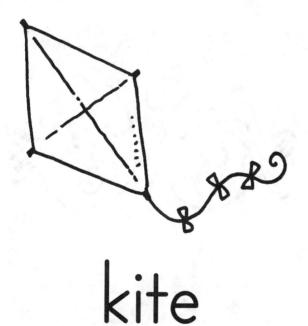

8

Reading Success Mini-Books: Initial Consonants   Scholastic Professional Books

# My Book of Words Beginning with Kk

Name _____

1

## kite

6

## kettle

3

# kangaroo

2

# kitten

7

# king

4

# kiss

5

## Match-up!

lamp

leaf

ladder

leg

lion

lemon

8

Reading Success Mini-Books: Initial Consonants   Scholastic Professional Books

# My Book of Words Beginning with Ll

Name _____

1

lemon

6

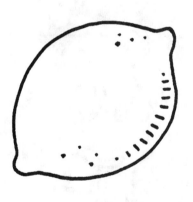

lamp

3

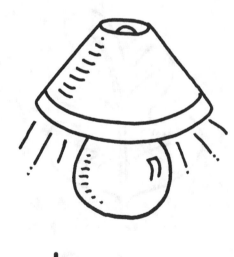

# ladder

2

# lion

7

# leaf

4

# leg

5

## Match-up!

mat

mouse

man

map

monkey

mask

8

Reading Success Mini-Books: *Initial Consonants*   Scholastic Professional Books

# My Book of Words
# Beginning with **Mm**

Name _____

1

## mouse

_____

6

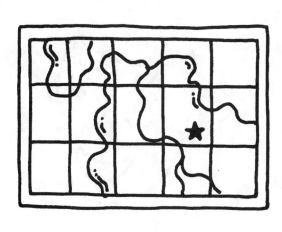

## map

_____

3

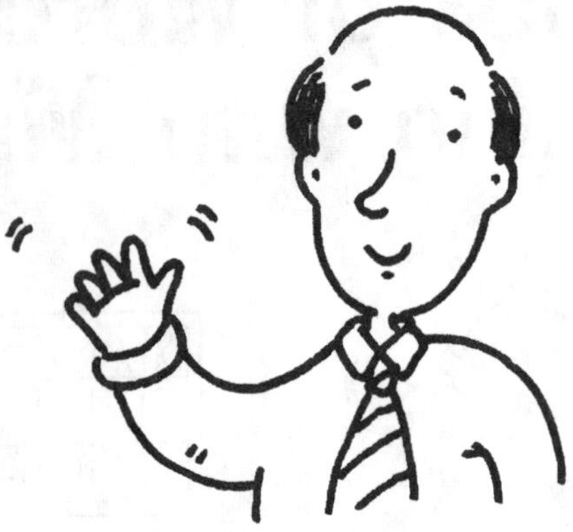

man

2

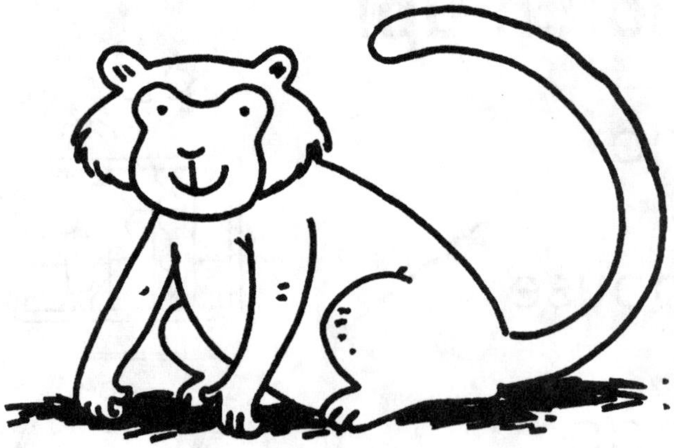

monkey

7

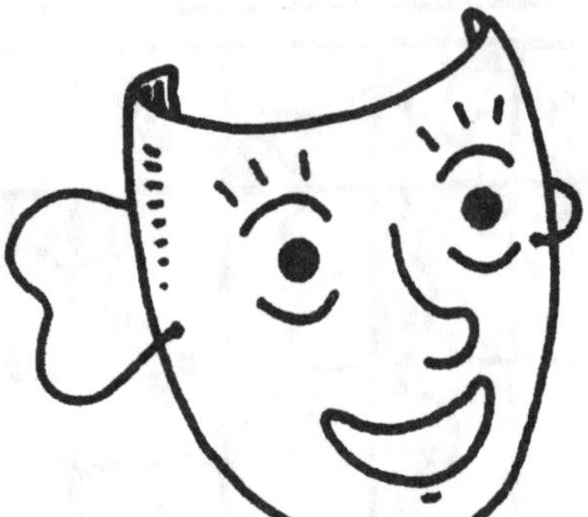

mask

4

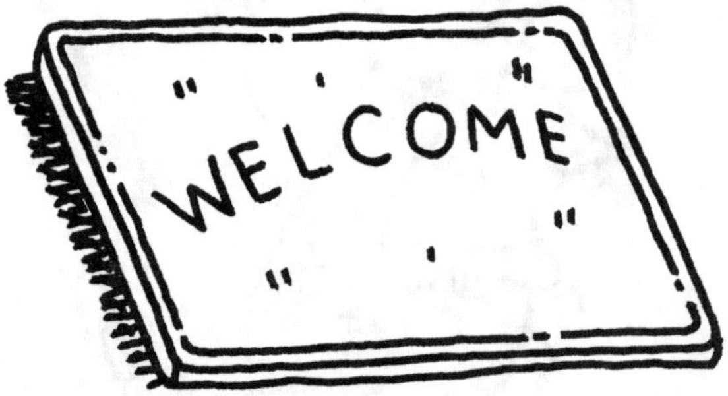


mat

5

# Match-up!

needle

nest

napkin

nut

nose

newspaper

8

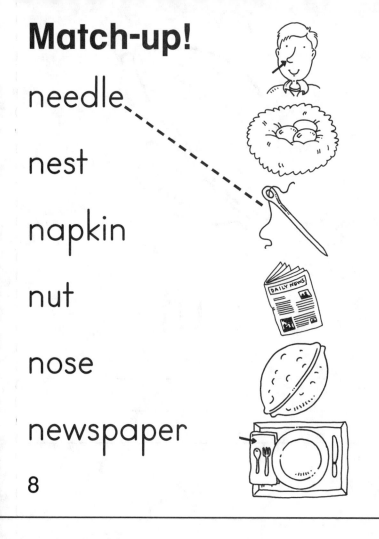

Name _____

Reading Success Mini-Books: Initial Consonants    Scholastic Professional Books

1

## nose

6

## needle

3

# napkin

---

2

# nut

---

7

# nest

---

4

# newspaper

---

5

# Match-up!

peas

pencil

pan

pillow

paints

pail

8

Reading Success Mini-Books: Initial Consonants    Scholastic Professional Books

# My Book of Words Beginning with Pp

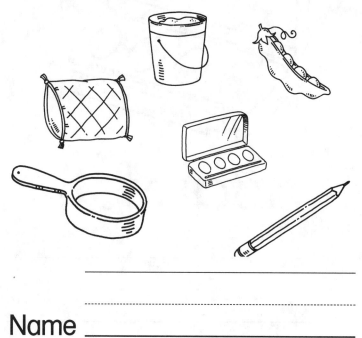

Name _____

1

# pencil

6

# pan

3

## paints

2

## pillow

7

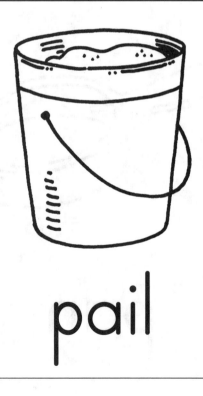

## pail

4

## peas

5

## Match-up!

quilt

queen

quake

quack

quiet

question

8

*Reading Success Mini-Books: Initial Consonants* Scholastic Professional Books

# My Book of Words Beginning with Qq

Name _____

1

## quiet

_____

_____

6

## quake

_____

_____

3

## quack

2

## quilt

7

## queen

4

## question

5

# Match-up!

radio

robe

rabbit

rope

rocket

roof

8

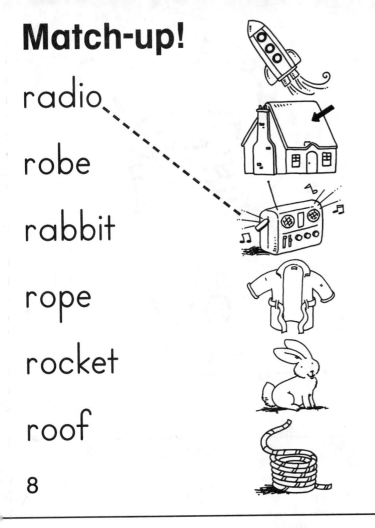

Reading Success Mini-Books: Initial Consonants    Scholastic Professional Books

# My Book of Words
# Beginning with Rr

Name _____

1

roof

_____

6

radio

_____

3

rabbit

_____

2

rope

_____

7

robe

_____

4

rocket

_____

5

# Match-up!

seven

saw

soap

seal

sandwich

sock

8

Reading Success Mini-Books: Initial Consonants   Scholastic Professional Books

# My Book of Words
# Beginning with **Ss**

Name _____

1

## soap

_____

6

## saw

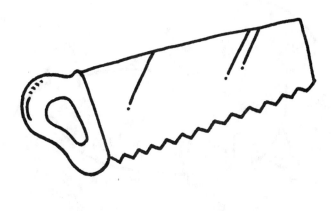

_____

3

## sandwich

_____

2

## sock

_____

7

## seal

_____

4

## seven

_____

5

## Match-up!

tub

tent

table

teddy

tire

toothbrush

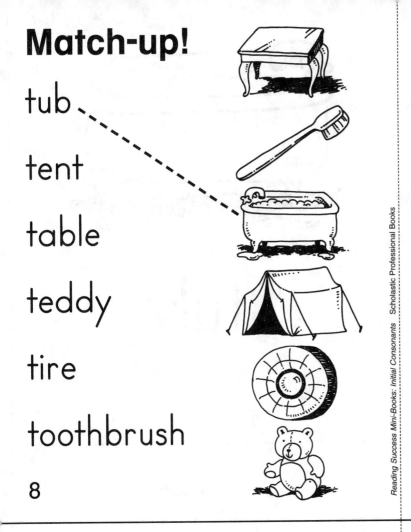

8

Reading Success Mini-Books: Initial Consonants   Scholastic Professional Books

# My Book of Words Beginning with Tt

Name _____

1

# toothbrush

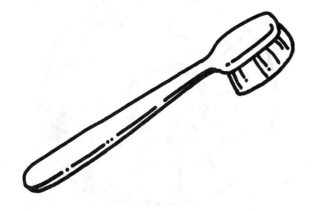

_____

_____

6

# tent

_____

_____

3

## table

2

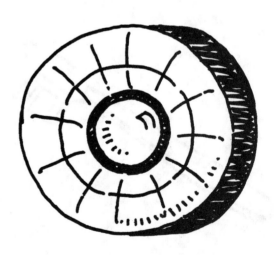

## tub

7

## teddy

4

## tire

5

# Match-up!

vest

van

violin

vane

vase

valentine

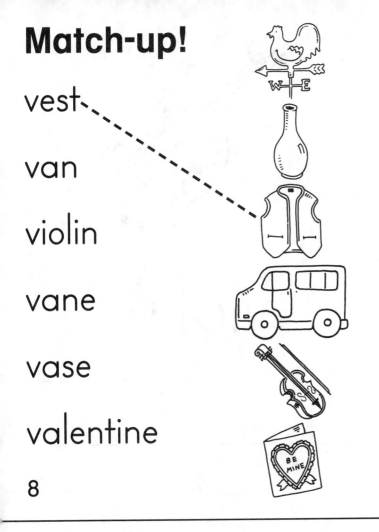

8

---

Reading Success Mini-Books: Initial Consonants    Scholastic Professional Books

# My Book of Words Beginning with **Vv**

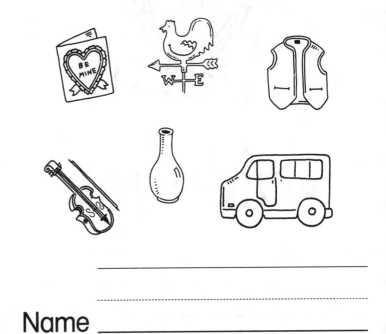

_____

Name _____

1

---

## vest

_____

_____

6

---

## van

_____

_____

3

# valentine

2

# violin

7

# vane

4

# vase

5

# Match-up!

wagon

web

wig

watch

worm

window

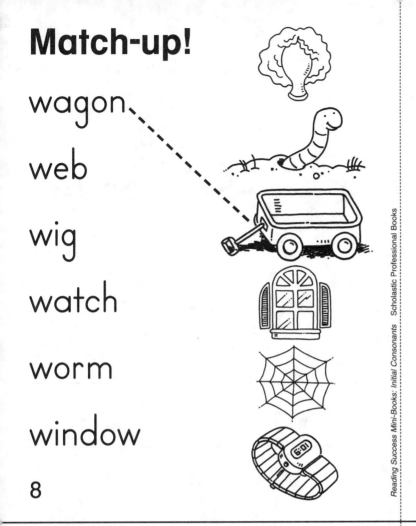

8

# My Book of Words Beginning with **Ww**

Reading Success Mini-Books: Initial Consonants   Scholastic Professional Books

Name _____

1

# window

6

# watch

3

# wagon

2

# worm

7

# web

4

# wig

5

# Match-up!

yo–yo

yarn

yak

yard

yolk

yam

8

# My Book of Words
# Beginning with Yy

Reading Success Mini-Books: Initial Consonants    Scholastic Professional Books

Name _____

1

## yolk

_____

6

## yam

_____

3

# yak

# yo-yo

# yard

# yarn

# Match-up!

zebra

zoo

zipper

zero

zone

zigzag

8

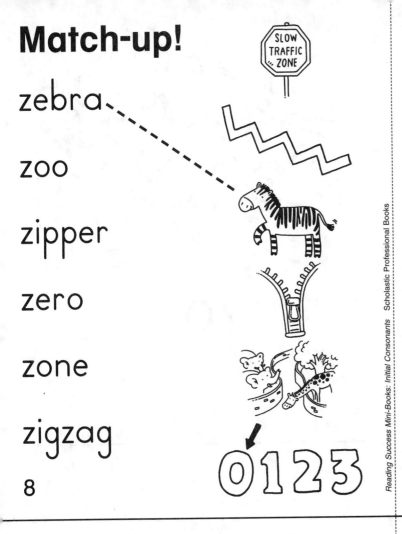

Reading Success Mini-Books: Initial Consonants    Scholastic Professional Books

# My Book of Words Beginning with **Zz**

Name _____

1

---

# zone

_____

6

---

# zero

_____

3

## zebra

2

## zoo

7

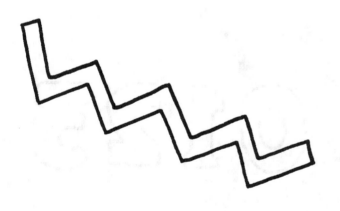

## zigzag

4

## zipper

5